DRYING FLOWERS

WORLD ✠ OF ✠ CRAFTS

DRYING FLOWERS

Barbara Radcliffe Rogers

Principal Photographer
Bruce McCandless

Friedman Group

A FRIEDMAN GROUP BOOK

ISBN 0-792-45299-2

WORLD OF CRAFTS: DRYING FLOWERS
was prepared and produced by
Michael Friedman Publishing Group, Inc.
15 West 26th Street
New York, New York 10010

Editor: Sharyn Rosart
Art Director: Jeff Batzli
Designer: Lynne Yeamans
Photography Editor: Christopher Bain
Illustrator: Madeline Sorel

Typeset by The Interface Group, Inc.
Color separations by Kwongming Graphicprint Co.
Printed and bound in Hong Kong by Leefung-Asco Printers Ltd.

DEDICATION

To Terry and Doug—Whom I would have chosen as friends if good fortune had not made them family.

AUTHOR'S ACKNOWLEDGMENTS

Dried flower arrangements and crafts are essentially decorations, and like any ornament, they should not only enhance a setting, but be enhanced by it. Nowhere could the arrangements in this book be shown off more perfectly than in the 200-year-old John Hancock Inn in Hancock, New Hampshire. Its own decor, full of eclectic antiques, provided the right setting for each piece in turn.

My appreciation to Pat and Glynn Wells, innkeepers and long-time friends, for opening their home, as well as their inn, to us for photography. Always good humored, even as they tripped over electric cords and squeezed past tripods, they were the consummate innkeepers and gracious hosts throughout.

My appreciation to Sharyn Rosart, the editor whose close attention to detail extended to every phase of the book's production and whose unfailing good humor made the project easier and more enjoyable for everyone.

And to my family, Dee, Tim, Julie and Lura, each of whom is involved in the growing, harvesting, and use of our flowers, my biggest thank-you of all.

CONTENTS

INTRODUCTION
page 9

PART ONE:
PREPARATIONS
page 11

Growing Flowers
to Dry
page 12

Best Flowers
to Dry
page 14

Some
Additional Flowers
to Dry
page 17

Air Drying Fresh
Cut Flowers
page 23

Other Methods of
Plant Preservation
page 24

Buying Dried
Flowers
page 26

Tools and Supplies
page 29

PART TWO:
DRIED FLOWER
PROJECTS
page 35

A Basket of
Field Flowers
page 37

A Williamsburg
Fan Arrangement
page 41

A Window Basket
Arrangement
page 45

A Wreath of
Artemisia
page 47

Wreath
Everlastings
page 50

Braided Raffia
Wreath
page 53

Dried
Flower Swag
page 57

Dried Flower
Bouquet
page 59

Small Bouquet

page 63

Hanging Bunches
of Flowers

page 66

Braided Garland

page 69

A Flower Braid

page 73

A Flowered
Straw Hat

page 75

A Flower-Trimmed
Basket

page 79

A Flowered Fan

page 83

A Potpourri Box

page 85

A Valentine Box

page 87

A Ball of
Flowers

page 91

A Flower
Crown

page 93

Hair Nosegays

page 97

An Artemisia Tree

page 101

Christmas
Nosegays

page 105

Tiny Tussie-Mussies

page 109

Strawflower
Tussie for the Tree

page 113

Tiny Tree Bouquets

page 115

Walnut Shell
Ornaments

page 117

Dried Flower
Potpourri

page 119

SOURCES

page 125

INDEX

page 126

Dried flowers retain their colors and textures, and often, their scents, to bring the beauty of these blooms into your home year-round.

INTRODUCTION

So brief is the life of a blooming flower, it is no wonder that we strive to preserve it to brighten our rooms during bleak seasons. The work began centuries ago, when herbs and flowers were hung to dry for their medicinal and cosmetic values. Somewhere in these early stillrooms, it was perhaps noticed that some of the dried blossoms retained their shape and color.

By the era we know as Victorian, the procedures for drying plant material had risen to a fine art, and we are still very much influenced by the methods and styles of that period.

Now that gardening is among the most popular leisure activities and fashion trends have reawakened an interest in things Victorian and Edwardian, everlasting plants are enjoying a revival. No longer are flower crafts the exclusive domain of the lady of leisure; men and women of all ages and interests are growing, buying, preserving, and creating beautiful decorations with flowers.

One small book can never hope to cover all there is to know about drying flowers, let alone give instructions for every possible craft and decoration that makes use of them. The short gardening section, "Growing Flowers to Dry," is intended as a guide for beginners. Those without the time, space, or interest to grow their own everlasting flowers may wish to skip over this information entirely.

For the person who enjoys creating beautiful things, the projects in this book will serve only as an introduction. Once the basics are mastered and the feel of handling dried plants is a familiar one, original creations will spring forth easily. Each plant seems to suggest its own use, colors seem to group themselves artistically, and the design process becomes second nature.

Nature, after all, is what this book is all about. To bring a piece of the natural world inside and preserve it to enjoy for many months is the goal of everyone who works with drying flowers.

PART ONE

Preparations

GROWING FLOWERS TO DRY

Choosing the right flowers to grow is the first step. The best for craft use are those that can be air-dried and will retain their shape, color, and natural look. As well as being the best for preserving, these flowers are also dependable in the garden.

Start the seeds in long plastic trays divided into inch-wide (2.5 cm) rows, which sit suspended in deeper solid plastic trays that hold water. Use a sterile starting medium, such as Jiffy-Mix™, that is fine and light in texture and will hold the necessary moisture without becoming soggy and drowning the tiny sprouts. A fine-grained starter mix will also be important when it comes time to separate the tender roots and move them to individual pots.

Pour the dry soil mix into the long rows, filling each to within a quarter inch (6 mm) of the top. Shake the trays gently to settle, but not pack, the mix, and add more if needed. Tap seeds gently onto the soil, trying to avoid clumping them, and spread with your fingers until there are about 8 to 10 to the inch (2.5 cm). Since some seeds are tiny, it is almost impossible to get them evenly spread, and it is not necessary to try.

According to the light needs of each type of flower—read the packets carefully to learn what these are—cover the seeds with as much as a quarter inch (6 mm) of starter mix. Set the seed trays into the solid trays that are half-filled with luke-warm water.

It is important to remember to label the plants, not only to know their names, but to know where to put them in the garden. Be sure to use a waterproof marker and a plastic or other permanent tag; paper labels will not withstand frequent watering. Keep trays in a well lit and moderately warm place.

When the seedlings are 1 to 2 inches (2.5 to 5 cm) tall, move them to individual pots, carefully separating the roots. Put two or three in each pot, unless the seeds are very precious or germination is poor. When this is the case, it is better to use up a pot for a weak seedling than to waste a possible plant. Again use the plastic pots

that are attached in rows and fit into the same large plastic base trays for watering. The labels now move with the plants. When plants are well started and have developed true leaves, cut off all but the strongest plant in each pot, clipping with scissors instead of pulling in order to avoid disturbing the roots of the remaining plant.

When the nights become warmer, close to your local last frost date, begin "hardening off" the plants by taking them outdoors during the middle of the day, later leaving them out all day and bringing them in only at night. At this point begin watering them from above with a sprayer.

When plants are sturdy and the risk of frost is over, transplant them to the garden, planting each where it will look and perform the best. Plant plume celosia, globe amaranth, and others that continue to bloom after the first picking in ornamental beds and annual borders.

© Sharon Guynup

Flowers for drying can be grown in almost any flower garden, from formal settings to casual clumps along the barn wall.

Perennials such as yarrow and tansy fit well in permanent flower beds, since they either continue to bloom after harvest or at least have attractive foliage. Whatever their other individual needs, everlastings almost universally need plenty of sun and space to grow and flower abundantly.

Once the plants are in the garden, caring for them simply means keeping them well watered and weed-free. There is very little special care involved, such as pruning or pinching out tips, and insect pests are rarely a problem with these tough descendants of the wild plants of the South African and Australian bush.

Harvesting is different for each plant, but most should be picked when they are just short of full bloom. This is because they continue to mature for a time after harvest. If you wait until full bloom, they will be overmature by the time they begin to dry. Watch carefully, checking plants each morning, when they begin to bloom, since many open very quickly once they start.

The best time of day to harvest is late in the morning, when the plants are completely dry of dew but have not yet begun to droop from the afternoon sun. Some, like statice, can be picked every few days; but others, such as strawflowers, need to be harvested daily since they overbloom quickly.

Bring all flowers indoors (or onto a shady porch) for processing immediately (*see* "Air Drying Fresh Cut Flowers," page 23), since they should not be left in tight bundles or piled in baskets for more than a few minutes. Although they are sturdy when dry, the blossoms are surprisingly fragile when they are fresh, and they crush easily.

Yarrow

Achillea
(Yarrow)

The yellow varieties produce large, flat heads of tiny blossoms on plants that may be 3 feet (90 cm) tall. The red and pink varieties are not as tall and have smaller flowers. All the varieties grow mounds of fernlike foliage that spread moderately each year. This is a good per-ennial to place in the rear of a permanent flower bed.

Harvest yarrow by cutting near the base of the stem, just as all the little florets are barely open. These can be dried upright standing loosely in a vase or suspended through wire mesh. Individual heads may be hung upside down, rather than tying them in bundles, which tends to crush the flower heads.

Artemisia
('Silver King' or 'Silver Queen')

These tall, branching perennials are used for their gray-green foliage, which makes a beautiful base for herb wreaths. They grow as tall as 4 feet (120 cm) and spread quickly from underground runners, so when planting, consider giving these plants a bed to themselves.

Harvest at any time for the foliage, and hang in bundles to dry. The most attrac-tive stage of artemisia has erect spikes of the beadlike blossoms. Harvest after these have formed, but before a hard frost. At this stage it can be dried stand-ing up in a vase or basket, but be careful to give it enough room so that it doesn't crush together as it dries. For wreaths, artemisia should be used while it is fresh and pliable.

Artemisia

Celosia
(Plume Celosia)

Feathery plume celosia comes in a variety of vivid colors ranging from pale cream and yellow through deep, russet orange and from pale pink through deep crimson. If the early annual flower plumes are cut off, the plants will produce subsequent crops of smaller heads on branching stems. This is an attractive addition to the annual border.

To dry plume celosia, lay it on its side on a screen. If this flower is dried hanging, moisture from its fleshy stems will drain into the blossoms, damaging both color and shape.

Globe Amaranth

Plume Celosia

Gomphrena
(Globe Amaranth)

One of the less well known everlastings, globe amaranth has an abundance of blossoms that look like compact red clover heads. They come in white, pink, and rich red-purple and can be planted with other annuals in borders or in rows in the cutting garden.

Pick individual stems as the flowers mature. They have a very long "vine life" and hold their color well. To dry, hang in bundles. You may have to replace the natural stems with wire, since they sometimes become very brittle when they dry.

Gypsophila
(Baby's breath)

Great clouds of tiny white or pink blossoms turn this perennial into a white shrub when it is in full bloom. Because of its size (up to 4 feet [120 cm]) it may need to be staked to prevent it from falling over, and it is usually planted at the end of a perennial bed.

Since the plants often bloom in sections, cut each stem when about three-fourths of its flowers are fully opened, the rest still in bud stage. Hang each stem separately to dry. The best way to hang it is to run a string through the lower branches and hang each clump like a giant tumbleweed.

Helichrysum
(Strawflower)

Probably the best known of all the everlastings, this annual is a rangy plant that grows as tall as 5 feet (150 cm). Colors range from white and yellow to orange and brown and through all the shades of pink and red. It is usually sold in mixed flats. Dwarf varieties are attractive in annual borders or mixed with marigolds or zinnias.

Harvest by cutting each flower head individually at its base. Place on wire stems by pushing the end of a wire into the soft base where the stem was cut, and dry by standing it upright in a vase or basket. As the flower dries, it closes tightly around the wire, securing it in place.

Strawflower

Annual Statice

Limonium
(Statice)

Second only to the strawflower in popularity, this sturdy annual is available in beautiful shades of blue and purple, as well as pink, white, and yellow. Perennial forms have tiny flowers in pale lavender and white. Stems of both annuals and perennials are quite sturdy and hold their shape when dried upright. Either is best planted in the cutting garden.

Harvest entire stems when the flowers are fully bloomed, but have not yet begun to fade. They can be tied in clumps and either hung or massed upright in vases to dry. Be very careful handling the dry flowers, since they fall off easily. If this should happen while you are working with them, you can replace the fallen blossom with a touch of glue.

Physalis
(Chinese Lantern)

Be careful where you plant this sprawling plant, since it spreads quickly and invades neighboring beds. But it is well worth growing for its papery orange lanterns. Try putting this perennial in a bed of its own, away from other flower gardens.

Pick after the lanterns have turned bright orange, or they will shrivel before drying. Hanging these is always a problem because the vines are so straggly—if hung upside down, the stems stiffen with the pods pointing upward. However, since the flowers are usually removed from the vine before use anyway, this is still the best way to dry the plant.

Chinese Lantern

SOME ADDITIONAL FLOWERS TO DRY

In addition to the most common and easily grown everlastings described in Chapter One, there are other suitable plants that can also be grown, purchased, or gathered in the wild. The following are used or mentioned for some of the projects in this book.

© Derek Fell

Heather

Agrostis, Briza, Eragrostis, and Panicum
(Grasses)

Along with grains—such as rye, wheat, and oats—which may be purchased already dried, there are many wild grasses with attractive heads for dried flower crafts. The roadside is often the best place to shop for these.

Anaphalis margaritacea
(Pearly Everlasting)

Although this plant grows in some places as a common roadside weed, if it is picked it often fails to regenerate. Therefore it is better to buy this plant from commercial growers. The small, pure white flowers can be replaced with the larger varieties of baby's breath for most uses.

Calluna vulgaris
(Heather)

The pink spikes of tiny, beadlike flowers of this plant dry easily and retain their color. Hang heather upside down to dry.

Dusty Miller

Centaurea rutifolia or Senecio cineraria
(Dusty Miller)

Used in annual flower beds and formal borders, this gray foliage plant is usually purchased at nurseries, and it grows easily. The thick, furry leaves are almost white and have a delicate, lacy cut edge. It can be dried easily by pressing between sheets of paper.

Cortaderia argentea
(Pampas Grass)

The tall white or pink plumes of this grass are usually grown in clumps. The plumes are so large that they frequently have to be broken into smaller segments and wired to stems before using.

Daveus carota
(Queen Anne's Lace)

This is a common weed and roadside flower with large, flat, white blossoms. When dried, its umbels close into a pale green cluster that is very striking in arrangements.

Pampas Grass

African Daisy

Filipendula hexapetala
(Meadowsweet)

This roadside shrub has spikes of fluffy pink flowers in the summer. Gather these and stand or hang them to dry. They will darken as they dry, but they make nice accents in arrangements.

Gnaphalium
(Fairy Gold)

Also known as annual achillea, this low-growing plant has clusters of small, bright yellow buttons.

Helipterum roseum, H. manglesii
(African Daisy)

Most florists and seed houses continue to sell the African daisy under its old botanic classification, *Acrolinium*. To further confuse you, others call it *Rhodanthe*! Its small, daisylike flowers in pink and white have yellow centers. It can be grown from seed or nursery plants. The stems tend to be very brittle, so they are usually replaced by very thin florist wire.

Lavender

Lavandula officinalis
(Lavender)

This woody perennial herb has spikes of very fragrant tiny purple blossoms. Dried on the stem, lavender can be used in small arrangements, but is most often used in potpourri.

Origanum vulgare
(Marjoram)

The culinary herb, sweet marjoram, has pale and insignificant blossoms, but the wild, or "pot," marjoram grows taller and has deep rose to purple blooms that dry beautifully. The stems are sturdy, and the flowers may be dried standing in a dry vase or basket.

Pot Marjoram

Roses

Rosa rugosa, R. centifolia, R. multiflora
(Roses)

The old June-blooming varieties are the kind most often used for craft work, since they retain their sweet fresh scent. When larger roses are needed for special projects, they can be purchased from florist suppliers, but keep in mind that these are not very fragrant. In this book all the roses called for are the tiny dried rosebuds sold by potpourri suppliers. If you are fortunate enough to obtain these roses fresh, snip them as closed buds, leaving about an inch (2.5 cm) of stem attached. Dry them in the shade, scattered on screens. Pick full-blown roses, too, and dry the petals for potpourri.

Lambs' Ears

Tanacetum vulgare
(Tansy)

An old-fashioned garden perennial, tansy grows wild, especially near the ocean. Its bright yellow buttons grow in clusters on tall stems. Pick them just before they are fully bloomed and dry by hanging.

Tansy

Solidago sempervirens
(Goldenrod)

Abundant in vacant lots and fields throughout much of North America, goldenrod should be picked before it is in full bloom to keep the heads from shattering as they dry.

Stachys olympica
(Lambs' Ears)

Also called woolly betony, this is a perennial that can be purchased from herb farms. The large, oblong leaves are light gray-green, soft, and furry. Rosettes of the leaves are used on wreaths and in arrangements by attaching them to florist picks while they are still fresh and not yet brittle.

AIR DRYING FRESH CUT FLOWERS

When drying most of the "natural everlastings," hanging them upside down in a shaded, airy, dry place with plenty of room between them is sufficient. Color and shape keep best when the flowers dry quickly, so it is important to keep bundles small, loose, and well spaced. Flowers that are crushed together in bundles for drying will be pushed into unnatural shapes and once they are dry, will be hard to separate without breaking. Tie with elastic bands since they tighten as the stems dry and shrink.

The only reason for hanging flowers is to keep the stems at right angles to the flower heads, the natural position in which they grow. Many flowers, if left standing, lose strength in the upper stem as they dry. When this happens, the heavy flower head falls over and dries facing downward—a very unattractive form for arranging.

Some flowers with stiff stems and light heads, such as statice, can be dried standing up in a vase or basket. To keep from crushing them together, place a sheet of chicken or rabbit fencing over the top of a large can, and stand the flowers by inserting their stems through the holes. Flowers with spindly or weak stems or heads too wide to be bundled can also be suspended through the holes of a large sheet of chicken or rabbit fencing with the flowers supported by the screen and stems hanging below.

Choosing a space for hanging flowers is similar to selecting a place to grow them in the garden: It depends largely upon what space is available. Light is not a problem as long as it isn't direct sunlight. You can string lengths of stout cord or clothesline along the ceiling of a covered porch and hang bundles of flowers using clip clothespins.

Once they are dried, store the flowers in a hanging position or standing in baskets. Delicate blues and pinks keep their color best in the dark, or at least in a dim light, but beware of keeping them in boxes because they can absorb moisture from the air and eventually mildew. Large bundles may be left hanging until needed in a barn loft or dry attic or shed as long as there is good air circulation. Although they are pretty hanging in the kitchen, do this for decoration only, never putting any there that you will need for future use. Steam carries a residue of cooking oils that coats the flowers and makes dust cling to them.

When working with dried flowers, and even just moving them from place to place, you will inevitably lose little bits. Tiny blossoms break off brittle stems, and sometimes a flower will burst apart in a shower of loose petals. Carefully gather and save these remnants in a jar, then add the dried petals of roses and other fragrant flowers and herbs to create an easy potpourri.

OTHER METHODS OF PLANT PRESERVATION

While those plants commonly known as "everlastings" are air-dried, there are other flowers and foliage that are preserved using various different methods.

WATERING

Sometimes a flower or leaf needs to be dried slowly in order to preserve its color or shape, so it is placed in a vase or other container with about 2 inches (7 cm) of water. As the water evaporates, the stems absorb a little of it, thereby slowing the drying process. When using the watering method, be sure that all stems reach the bottom of the container so that they can obtain water.

PRESSING

Nearly everyone has, at some time, saved a flower or a leaf by pressing it between the pages of a book. While wooden flower presses capable of holding many layers of plants are available, an old telephone directory is still one of the most commonly used presses. Arrange flower petals and leaves carefully as you close the book to be sure they are spread and not folded. Larger foliage and entire branches of leaves can be dried between sheets of newsprint. These heavier materials do not require tight pressing as do more delicate blossoms; a light weight, such as a piece of Masonite or plywood, will do. Papers should be porous, not coated and shiny.

SAND

While this is another very common and effective drying procedure, it is not the easiest. It is used by those who wish to do it in the authentic early American method or who wish to avoid the expense of silica gel. Choice and correct preparation of the sand is vital. By far the best is the oolitic sand from the shores of the Great Salt Lake in Utah. Instead of sharply fractured particles of stone, it is composed of tiny, waterworn fragments of fine shell. Each grain is round, so no damage is done to tender petals, and its chemical makeup helps to preserve natural colors. Lacking this, a fine, clean beach sand may be used, but it must first be washed thoroughly by stirring it around in large amounts of water several times.

To dry flowers, choose a container a little larger than the plant material and begin with 1 inch (2.5 cm) of dry sand. Place the flower or flowers on it and dribble a stream of dry sand over it to fill all the crevices and support its outer sides. The goal is to cover it completely without changing its shape. Sometimes it is helpful to use a little funnel made of a rolled cone of paper to distribute sand in exactly the right places.

SILICA GEL

A commercial product, silica gel is quite expensive, so it should be used judiciously. Use a container very close to the plant's size and shape that can be sealed tightly. (Silica gel absorbs moisture from the air just as readily as from the plants, so a tight seal is important for quick drying.) Follow the same procedure as for drying with sand. Since it takes only a few days, silica gel can be reused quickly. When the little blue crystals turn pink, they have absorbed all the moisture they can hold. To be reused, they need to be baked in a slow oven (that is, at the lowest setting) and spread in a thin layer, until they turn blue again. Be sure to cool them before use. Since this dessicant works quickly, it is especially good for fragile plants and those with delicate colors.

GLYCERIN

The large sprays of leaves with a very pliable but slightly leathery feel that are often found in florists shops are preserved in glycerin. This is an improvement over the more brittle, flattened sprays of pressed leaves, but glycerin takes its toll on color. Greens preserved with glycerin become brown, bronze, or even black, depending on the amount of time they spend in the solution. Foliage preserved in this manner must be near the middle of its growth season; the method will not work with tender, early leaves or late, dry ones, and it will not preserve autumn foliage colors.

To use this method, mix one part glycerin with three parts very hot water. Cut a deep split in the base of any heavy, woody stems and stand stems in 3 inches (7.5 cm) of the solution. Leave the plants until the foliage is leathery or has reached the desired color. If glycerin droplets appear on the foliage, wipe these off carefully before using the plants in arrangements.

BUYING DRIED FLOWERS

Even those dedicated gardeners who grow rows of flowers for drying buy special flowers that grow only in other climates. Those without gardens must buy all their dried material.

The easiest plants to find are strawflowers, statice, and baby's breath. The last mentioned two are used fresh by florists in great quantity. You can buy them and dry them yourself (or, if you are lucky enough to receive flowers often, keep them after the bouquet fades). Even after standing in a vase of water for a week, statice dries well and keeps its color.

Most florists carry bunches of strawflowers. They are also available at hobby shops, farm stands, and farmers' markets. These are good places to look for other flowers as well, particularly in the fall. Herb farms also often have dried flowers for sale.

Hobby shops may carry them, but they are often dyed garish colors—vivid blues, reds, and purples. There are times when a little touch of a bright red or orange is effective in craft work, but such shades more often detract from the natural beauty you've tried so hard to achieve.

Herb and potpourri suppliers and some health-food stores with bulk herbs and spices carry dried, whole rosebuds. You may have to buy these mixed with fragrant rose petals and sort them out yourself—a pleasant job. Save the petals for potpourri.

Uva ursi leaves and whole bay leaves, also found at herb and potpourri shops, are perfect for foliage in dried flower crafts. These leaves are tiny and a nice shade of green, as well as being well shaped and sturdy.

If you are unable to find dried flowers locally, there are firms that ship them by mail. You can either buy bunches of one kind of flower or mixed bouquets that can be used in a variety of projects. See Sources, page 125, for addresses.

TOOLS AND SUPPLIES

Most of the materials needed for working with dried flowers are common household items or are readily available at craft and hardware stores. There are no special or single-purpose tools required. The following list explains the uses and compares the merits of a number of the materials and tools mentioned in the projects.

SCISSORS AND WIRE CUTTERS

It is a good idea to have on hand an old pair of scissors for cutting thin wires and plant stems, since this kind of use ruins good scissors. Pliers and a wire cutter can be used for stems as well as wire. You may want to keep a small pair of better scissors handy for such tasks as clipping threads, trimming raffia, and cutting ribbon.

WIRE

Florist wire is best for most projects, since it is available with a dark green enamel coating that blends in well with natural material. It comes on spools and in cut lengths and in a variety of gauges. The larger the gauge number, the finer the wire. Medium gauge is good for stems on smaller flowers and for those that must be bent easily. Heavy wire is harder to bend, but is preferable as stems of heavier flowers. Purchase the heavier gauges that you will use for stems in cut lengths instead of spools, to avoid the sometimes difficult task of straightening spooled wire.

There are several reasons to use wire stems on dried plant material. Many natural stems are simply too weak or too brittle when dried to hold up the heads of the flowers. Some flowers are too large (yarrow and plume celosia need to be broken apart for all but the largest arrangements or wreaths) while others are too small to show up alone. Wire stems also bend, allowing great flexibility in their placement. Yarrow, for example, faces upward, which is fine in a basket placed on the floor, but often lost in a table arrangement or on a swag.

Wiring also allows the designer to group flowers attractively. Three round

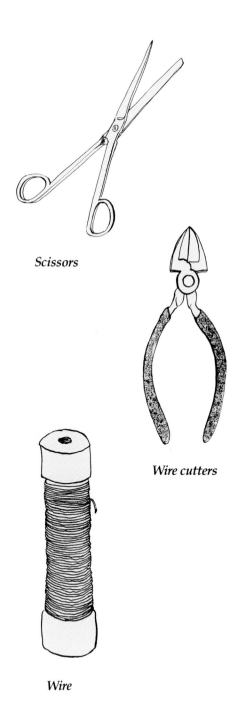

Scissors

Wire cutters

Wire

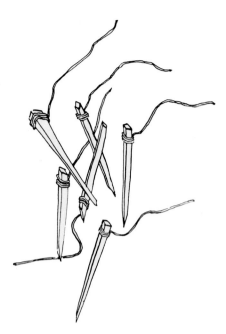

Florist picks

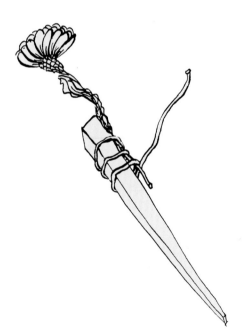

Wiring a stem to a florist pick

globe amaranth flowers can be staggered at slightly different heights, or statice colors can be combined in a cluster on a wreath.

In arrangements using sand or Oasis bases, wire stems slide more smoothly, take up less room, and are less likely to break off while they are being handled.

To wire a single flower onto a stem, cut the natural stem to about an inch (2.5 cm) long (more for very heavy flowers) and lay it beside the wire stem. Wrap the two together with florist tape, stretching it to activate its adhesive quality. Several smaller blossoms can be wired to a single stem in the same way, usually at staggered heights if they are to be used in a standing arrangement.

Large flowers that need to be broken up should be separated carefully, leaving as much natural stem on each piece as possible. Those bits with short stems can be saved for projects that require gluing. Long spikes of flowers can be grouped together so that the bottom part is not lost in a bouquet, while clumps of blossoms can be wired along the length of a stem to provide the longer lines needed in a swag.

FLORIST PICKS

Available in green or natural wood colors, florist picks look like fat toothpicks with a wire tail. The wire is very fine and wraps easily around even very small stems. Picks are used to give length or strength to flower stems when they are to be used in wreath making or other crafts in which they must be pushed into a base. The easiest way to attach a florist pick to a stem is to hold the stem and the pick together between the thumb and forefinger and roll them together. This will wrap the little wire tail tightly around the stem in one quick movement. Picks are also used to combine several small flowers into a bunch for use on wreaths or in miniature arrangements.

Florist picks are used much like wire stems, but the fine wire on their ends replaces the florist tape. Since picks are used in places where the blossoms are inserted straight up, such as on a wreath or into a base or frame, the wire wrapping is covered. In tiny nosegays, where picks hold small stems better than tape, the wire can be hidden by a single wrapping of tape.

BASES

With the discovery of the damaging effects of polystyrene upon the ozone layer of our atmosphere, conscientious craft workers have avoided its use in the form of Styrofoam™ products. Those who work with dried flowers have missed it the most. The round and cone-shaped forms were perfect for covering with dried blossoms to create hanging ornaments and table trees. Styrofoam™ wreath rings, while handy for some things, were not as hard to replace.

Round and Conic Bases

There are now several options for the balls. One is to use the hard plastic "eggs" that panty hose come in and attach flowers with a glue gun instead of pins. To create a sphere instead of an egg shape, glue two bottom halves together.

If you need a number of round bases and do not have a source of plastic eggs, make papier mâché balls by covering small balloons with strips of newspaper that have been dipped in a simple paste of flour and water. Hang these to dry by their "stems." When they are crisp-dry, pop the balloons with a pin and pull them out. Let the balls dry overnight, and seal the holes with a strip of paper dipped in paste. If you do a number of these at once, they take very little time. They cost almost nothing and can be painted easily. Glues of all kinds adhere to them.

Cone-shaped bases can be made from chicken wire, as directed in the "Artemisia Tree" project, page 100. These can be filled with moss or covered with a single layer of burlap to provide a more solid surface for gluing or inserting florist picks and stems.

Oasis bases are green soft foam bricks available from florists that are excellent for holding dried flowers in containers.

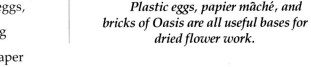

Plastic eggs, papier mâché, and bricks of Oasis are all useful bases for dried flower work.

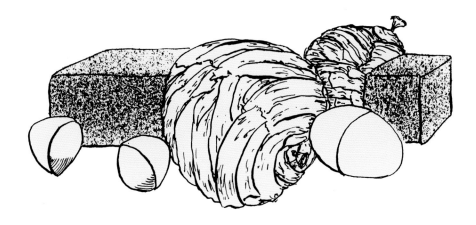

Straw wreath base

Braided raffia wreath base

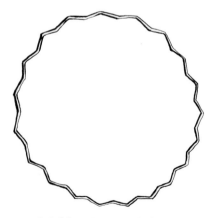

Crinkle-wire wreath frame

Wreath Bases and Frames

Straw wreath bases are good for some things, but they tend to be so tightly packed that stems, wires, and florist picks do not penetrate them. It is easier to make your own wreath base from a thick braid of raffia. Florist and hobby shops offer an interesting variety of wreath backings, including braided hemp and vines, most of which make good backgrounds for dried flower decorating.

For constructing your own wreaths of dried flowers you will need a wire ring called a "crinkle-wire wreath frame." These look like they are made of wire rick-rack, and this zigzag wire shape holds material firmly in place. These are quite inexpensive and available from florists.

ADHESIVES

The world of dried flower designers seems to be evenly split between those who never use a glue gun and those who wouldn't work without one. Somewhere between there is a happy medium. The advantage of a glue gun is that it aims a dot of glue accurately that dries almost instantly, remaining just pliable enough to hold dry material securely. There are projects, such as attaching flowers to the rim of a basket, that do require this instant drying ability.

The disadvantages are that the gun is often awkward to use on small projects. It also leaves a web of little plastic strings that must be cut off, and if not used carefully, it may create great globs of unsightly glue on the craft.

Wreath makers shun the glue gun, preferring to wire materials in place. Since a wreath is an airy, light creation, glue of any sort, except for tiny pieces and quick repairs, is not suitable. The major objection to the glue gun is that it interferes with the feeling of working with natural materials. When you have a hot machine in one hand, there is a sense of immediacy and less of an opportunity to experiment, which is half the fun of working with dried flowers. With a glue gun, once something is in place, it's there forever. Even the thick, quickset glues allow more leeway.

The best all-around glue for dried flower work is a thick white glue that "sets up" quickly and dries with some flexibility. Model cements become brittle and cannot withstand the slight movements of dried plants as they expand and contract in response to humidity changes. Rubber cement does not adhere well to plants and many other glues crack or peel. Although there may be other brands that work, I have found Aleene's Tacky Glue™ to dry fastest and clearest, hold things in place best. In the projects, it is listed simply as white glue, to save describing it each time.

In each of the projects that follow, the list of materials includes the best glue for specific uses.

FLORIST TAPE

Available in rolls from florist shops, this tape is made of a very thin paper that is not at all sticky as it comes off the roll, but becomes adhesive when stretched. This is a distinct advantage, since it sticks only where you need it—around the stem of a flower. It is used both to attach wires to flowers and to cover the wire on those that have been wired together. It also covers florist picks, which allows them to blend into a bouquet, as well as the handles of nosegays and tussie-mussies. It comes in many colors, but a medium to dark green is the best for most projects.

RAFFIA

Made from the raffia palm, this is one of the most versatile materials known to those who love the natural look of country crafts. Braided as a base for wreaths, garlands, or swags; employed as a wrapping; or used as a strong, natural tying cord, raffia is a basic supply with many, many uses. It is purchased from craft and hobby suppliers.

NYLON THREAD

Used to provide an invisible hanger for Christmas ornaments, nylon, or invisible, thread is available at fabric- and sewing-supply stores. Fine fishing leader can be used as well. Tying secure knots in this thread is difficult, so once tied, it is best to touch the knots with a tiny drop of glue on the end of a toothpick.

STRAIGHT PINS

Keep a box of these handy for anchoring dried flowers in place temporarily as you work. Once glued, flowers cannot be moved wthout damage. Some flowers can be pinned right through their centers, others through the petals, still others between the florets.

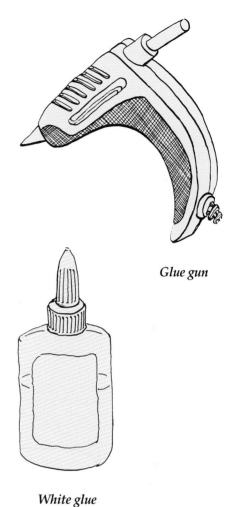

Glue gun

White glue

Raffia

PART TWO

Dried Flower
Projects

Opposite page: If wildflowers are not available, substitute other white, gold, and deep blue or purple flowers in the basket, but choose those with flat tops, not tall spikes to keep the symmetry of the arrangement. This page: Yarrow's large yellow blossoms are among the most popular for arrangements.

© Robert E. Lyons

A BASKET OF FIELD FLOWERS

Even this most informal and casual of dried flower arrangements requires attention to the basics of design and color. This Appalachian melon basket filled with flowers whose not-too-distant origins are in the fields and roadsides looks almost fresh. In fact, it almost could be arranged fresh, since most of the flowers in it can be dried standing up.

Materials:

- Melon basket
- Oasis block
- Fine-gauge florist wire
- Yarrow—about 30 heads of yellow flowers
- Statice—about 30 dark blue or purple clusters (wired to longer stems)
- Tansy—about 20 heads
- Goldenrod—about 30 heads
- Gnaphalium—about 24 heads (wired to longer stems)
- White or pale green flowers, such as Queen Anne's lace, meadowsweet, ammobium, or pearly everlasting—about 30 heads

Anchor the Oasis firmly into the bottom of the basket with a length of florist wire. Place clusters of yarrow in the Oasis, keeping the two sides of the basket balanced and the tops of the flowers about even with the height of the handle. Be sure to let some of the flowers extend over the sides of the basket. Next, add the statice, letting it stand a little above the yarrow in places. Fill in with the tansy and goldenrod, highlight with the gnaphalium, and finally, add wispy touches of the white or pale green material.

© Rogers Associates

A WILLIAMSBURG FAN
ARRANGEMENT

*Nowhere is the use of dried flowers to brighten the winter home exemplified
more beautifully than at Colonial Williamsburg, in Williamsburg, Virginia.
Grand mansions and simple houses are filled with dried arrangements, all
done in the authentic style of the period. • The type of flower holder used
in this arrangement was created for Queen Mary of England in the
seventeenth century, and its use quickly spread to the colonies. It is perfect for
the large and formal—yet exuberant—arrangements popular at that time.*

Materials:

- Fan vase with 5 holes (called fingers), filled with dry sand
- Magnolia leaves (treated with glycerin and wired and taped to longer stems)—9–10
- Goldenrod—about 12 heads
- Pampas grass—about 24 plumes
- Strawflowers in white and yellow shades—about 12 large and 12 small of each color (wired to longer stems)
- Statice—about 25 stems of blue flowers
- Strawflowers in dark red—about 12 very small flowers (grouped in clusters of 2 or 3 and wired to longer stems)
- Globe amaranth in white and orange shades—about 24 of each color (grouped in clusters of 2 or 3 and wired to longer stems)
- Tansy—about 12 small stems (grouped in clusters of 2 or 3 and wired to longer stems)
- Pearly everlasting or other white flower—about 24 clusters

You may not need all of this material, but it is wise to have enough on hand in case some breaks or is not the right size. Ultimately, the amount of material you need and the size of your arrangement depend on the size of the vase.

Arrange an uneven number of magnolia leaves in a fan shape at the back of the vase. These should be as tall as you wish to have your finished arrangement, since they form its background. The leaves at either end should point slightly downward, below the top of the vase. In front of the leaves, insert heads of goldenrod and pampas grass alternately, with one pampas plume in front of each magnolia leaf and goldenrod between them.

Moving forward and making each successive row shorter, fill in the yellow and white strawflowers until the arrangement is full and balanced, but not packed or crowded. Beginning at the back, and working evenly, intersperse heads of statice among the strawflowers, then highlight with the addition of red strawflowers.

© Rogers Associates

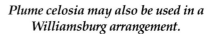
Finally, fill in with globe amaranth, tansy, and pearly everlastings, taking care to arrange the flowers so that they spill over the fingers at the bottom of the fan vase.

The beauty of wire stems in this arrangement lies in their flexibility: You can bend them to make the fan of flowers extend below the top of the vase. The other advantage is that wire moves more smoothly and takes up less room in a narrow-topped container.

A WINDOW BASKET ARRANGEMENT

Narrow windowsills never seem large enough to hold a normal flower arrangement, so this one is designed especially for a long, shallow space. The choice of flowers can change with the seasons or the color of the room. If the window is a sunny one, gold and yellow flowers will retain their colors better than pink, red, or blue ones. This arrangement is designed for the harvest time of year.

Materials:

- Cracker basket, long and narrow, designed for serving saltines
- Oasis or other soft floral base cut to fit the basket
- Strawflowers in yellow and gold shades on wire stems
- Statice in yellow shades
- Dried flowers in russet, brown, and orange shades
- Dried grasses, some with light, fluffy heads for filler

Begin with the larger strawflowers, placing them so that the ones in the center stand slightly taller than those on the outer edge. Bend their heads just barely forward. Add the smaller strawflowers, allowing at least one to trail over each end of the basket rim. Fill in with the statice and other flowers, keeping the design only slightly higher in the center and lower at the ends. Finally, fill in the spaces with grasses, adding a few in the back that are a little taller than the rest of the arrangement and some longer ones that trail at the ends.

© Derek Fell

A WREATH OF ARTEMISIA

An extremely attractive (and easy-to-make) dried decoration is the herbal wreath. Unlike evergreen wreaths, which are associated with the holiday season, those made of cornhusk or straw, which have autumnal tones, herb wreaths are "in season" at any time of year. • The easiest herbs to use for a wreath base are 'Silver King' or 'Silver Queen' artemisia. These tall herbs have narrow silver-green leaves and pliable stalks that bend easily to the shape of a wreath ring when they are fresh. If they have been dried, simply seal them in a large plastic bag overnight along with a well-dampened terry towel.

If you are right handed, begin with the first sprig facing left, with stems to the right.

Materials:

- Crinkle-wire wreath frame (wreath will be about twice the diameter of the frame)
- Pliable (preferably fresh) stems of artemisia
- Mediumweight florist wire
- Heavy scissors
- Florist picks
- Flowers for decorating (see box, "Wreath Everlastings")

Cut a long piece of florist wire, and twist one end around the wreath frame to secure it. Cut the bare or damaged portions off the bottoms of the artemisia stems and, beginning about 5 inches (12.5 cm) below the plant tip, wire 1 to the frame by wrapping the wire loosely around it once. Add another stem of artemisia to cover the first wire, and wrap it once or twice, working along the frame, bending the stems to follow the curve of the ring and leaving the leafy tips sticking out to form a fringe that will be the outer edge of the finished wreath.

Continue to add more stems, and secure them with wire along with the previous stems. As you work, the wreath base will form, consisting of a bundle of stems and the attached foliage. Do not wrap the wire too tightly, since the base needs space to hold the decorative material you will be adding later. The larger the wreath, the thicker the base should be in order for the plant material to remain in proportion.

When the base is completed, it can be hung to dry for later use, or it can be decorated immediately. Never stack bases to dry, because you will flatten the foliage.

When you are ready to complete the wreath, assemble all the dried decorative plants and flowers and group them by color. You can decide on a color scheme at the beginning, or you can experiment with various combinations as you go, simply trying the flowers and plants in different places. Do not apply any glue until you are happy with the arrangement.

The stems of the dried flowers should

Decorate a small wreath with flowers in one color range, in this case pinks, magentas, and purples.

be from 3 to 6 inches (7.5 to 15 cm) long. If they are too short, wire them to florist picks. Smaller flowers tend to get lost on large wreaths; they look better if grouped into clusters and wired together onto florist picks.

To attach the decorative flowers, simply push the stems or picks into the artemisia base or under the wrapping wire. If they seem loose, you can secure them with a drop or two of white glue.

In decorating, use the largest, bright-est, and heaviest flowers or seedpods first, as the focal points, and fill in with more delicate and less dramatic varieties. End with the wispy, fine plants such as baby's breath and peppergrass, which fill in spaces and lend an airy grace to the finished wreath.

It is a good idea to hang the wreath and look at it from across the room before considering it finished, since the balance of the shapes and colors shows up better at a distance.

Opposite page: After they are dried, most flowers can be stored in baskets or vases, decorating the house until they are needed for arrangements.

The most commonly available everlastings for wreaths are as follows:

White:

Strawflower, pearly everlasting, baby's breath, statice, globe amaranth, hydrangea.

Pink and purple:

Sea lavender, statice, pot marjoram, baby's breath, rosebud, pink yarrow, lavender, Scotch thistle.

Yellow and orange:

Strawflower, statice, goldenrod, marguerite, costmary, yarrow, celosia, Chinese lantern, tansy.

Red:

Strawflower, plume celosia, red rose, dock, globe amaranth, rosehips.

Green:

Bay leaf, lamb's ears, thyme, boxwood, germander, sage.

Brown:

Beebalm, wild iris, poppy, shepherd's purse, peppergrass, dock, other wild weeds and grasses.

Smaller wreaths usually look best with a limited range of colors, but larger ones can use many different colors effectively. Since the background foliage of artemisia is gray-green, using soft pinks and lavender shades makes a subtle and lovely combination. But even the brighter golds and russet tones look attractive, especially if they are accented by the darker browns of seedpods and natural buff shades of grasses.

Opposite page: A small braid of raffia provides the base for a small wreath to highlight a dry sink. This page: Plume celosia is a favorite of arrangers for its large plumes.

B R A I D E D   R A F F I A   W R E A T H

This small wreath is not intended for a front door, where it would be lost, but for a kitchen cabinet door or a small wall space. It would also be attractive hanging in a window, but for this use should be made with decorations on both sides.

Raffia is easy to braid, and can be made into a wreath by tying the ends together as shown.

Materials:

- Raffia bundle—at least 20 inches (50 cm) long and about half the amount you can grasp tightly in the circle made by your thumb and first finger
- Strawflowers in complementary colors
- Dried flowers of small size
- Dried grasses or flowers in spike shapes, such as artemisia and plume celosia
- White glue

Save 1 long, sturdy strand of raffia for tying, and match the ends of all the other strands fairly well so that the bundle is about the same thickness throughout. Tie it securely at one end with a small length of the reserved raffia.

Divide into thirds and braid loosely but evenly, making a fat, fairly flat braid. As you work, always pull the clump of raffia in your *right* hand a little tighter than the others. This will cause the braid to curve evenly and make it easier to form into a circle. Continue until braid forms a circle about 6 or 7 inches (about 15 cm) in diameter. Tie the second end.

Place one end over the other with the tails facing opposite directions so that they make a perfect circle. Tie the ends together securely with raffia, winding several times over an area of about an inch (2.5 cm). This will provide the base for your flower decorations, so be sure it is firm and stable.

Lay the wreath flat on your work surface and arrange the strawflowers, using the larger ones in the middle and keeping the colors balanced. Glue these in place when you have created an arrangement you like.

Fill in with the remaining flowers to make a grouping no larger than the bottom quarter of the circle. Add the grasses or spiky flowers at each end, curving upward along the wreath to finish off the design. Glue all these in place.

If the wreath is meant to hang in a window, wait until the glue has dried thoroughly, and at least overnight, before turning the wreath over and decorating the other side. The side that will face the glass should not use deep colors because they fade quickly in the sun.

DRIED FLOWER SWAG

Opposite page: A swag of dried flowers and artemisia hangs over the mirror in a guestroom of the Hancock Inn in Hancock, NH.

Dramatic as door decorations or in a wall space between windows, swags can also be used in pairs on mantels or above doorways. They are easier to make than wreaths, and the artemisia need not be either fresh or pliable.

Materials:

- Artemisia or dried grasses with long stems
- Dried flowers of various stem lengths, medium weight
- Florist wire
- Ribbon—at least a yard (90 cm) long and 1 inch (2.5 cm) wide for a large swag

Begin with several long stems of a foliage plant, such as artemisia or a bundle of tall grasses, and lay them on a flat surface, stems together. On top of these, lay shorter stalks of flowers, such as statice, stems even with the first group. Continue to fill in, using shorter-stemmed plants, until only the base stems show.

Tie these together into a firm bundle by wrapping several times with wire and cover the tie with a bow of appropriately colored ribbon. If the stems look too bare or the bow appears unbalanced, add some shorter sprigs of the same foliage or flowers, inserting them from the stem side into the ties.

Hang this simple but effective swag with the stem end upward.

For a symmetrical mantel decoration, make a pair of matching bundles, each half the length of the mantel, and tie the stem ends together. In place of a bow, cover the stems in the center with short-stemmed everlastings.

DRIED FLOWER BOUQUET

*Similar in construction to a swag, this bouquet can either be a freestanding
floral arrangement to decorate a table or a traditional gift. Gardeners
who grow dried flowers and wish to give them to friends for their own
projects often find this a more attractive way of presenting the gift than to
just pack all the flowers in a box. The bouquet itself can be enjoyed before it is
taken apart and used.*

Opposite page: Tiny bouquets are made in the same way as larger ones, but with smaller blossoms.

Begin with a bunch of shorter stemmed flowers and tie them in a bundle.

Materials:

- Assortment of long-stemmed dried flowers and grasses in a variety of colors and textures; strong, large flowers work better than fragile or delicate ones

- Fine-gauge florist wire

- Ribbon in an appropriate size and color for the flowers used

---

Gather a few stems of the shorter plant material together informally, and wrap with wire to secure. Continue to add flowers, wrapping with wire after each addition. Work upward, adding the flowers evenly to the sides and the back of the bouquet. Although the bouquet should be balanced for color and size, it should not be perfectly balanced. Try to achieve an informal effect as if the flowers had been gathered casually. When the bouquet has reached a size and shape that looks attractive to you, end the wire by twisting it around itself and cover the final wrapping with a ribbon tied in a bow.

This same method can be used to make smaller bouquets, which are lovely at individual place settings on a table or set on a table as an accent, much as you would place a small vase of flowers. To make smaller bouquets, use daintier flowers and smaller heads of grass. If you are using plume celosia in a small bouquet, separate it into smaller heads so that it will not dominate.

© Robert E. Lyons

SMALL BOUQUET

Nearly any dried flower can be used for this nosegay-style bouquet, but the
fragrance of pink roses adds to its charm. Real eyelet lace, gathered and glued
to the edge, can replace the doily.

Materials:

- Paper doily, about 6 inches (15 cm) in diameter
- 2 lengths medium-weight florist wire, each 12 inches (30 cm) long
- Cardboard circle, 4 inches (10 cm) in diameter
- White paper circle, 4 inches (10 cm) in diameter
- Masking tape
- Bottom half of a plastic egg
- Pink and white strawflowers, roses, gomphrena or other dried flowers
- Pink satin ribbon
- Floral tape
- Tacky glue or glue gun

Glue the paper circle to the cardboard. Bend wires in half and push ends through the center of the paper side of cardboard circle, about a half inch (1 cm) apart. Bend over a half inch (1 cm) of each wire end, like a staple, and secure to cardboard with masking tape. Glue the doily to the cardboard over the masking tape and wrap the wire "stem" completely in florist tape.

Center the plastic hemisphere on the doily and glue it in place. Cover this with dried flowers, first removing their stems and then gluing them to the plastic. Tie the ribbon in a bow with long streamers and glue it to one side of the top or tie it around the base of the stem on the underneath side.

HANGING BUNCHES OF FLOWERS

By far the easiest dried flower decorations, and among the most attractive in a country home, are simple bunches of dried flowers hanging from a rack or along a beam.

Flowers can be arranged in large or small bunches, and tied with jute cord, just as they were set to dry when harvested from the garden. In fact, the best way to bundle flowers is also the most attractive: those with longer stems in the middle and short-stemmed ones on the outside. If flowers are meant to hang against a wall, use long-stemmed flowers in the back and short-stemmed ones in front of each bunch, as you would make a swag.

If you are fortunate enough to have an old herb-drying rack, you can hang flowers and grasses on it and almost cover a wall with them. You might also use it as a divider in a large room.

Those without the space for such a rack, or enough flowers to fill it, can enjoy the same effect on a much smaller scale. Take a few sprigs of smaller dried flowers—such as gnaphalium, tansy, globe amaranth, ammobium, artemisia tips, or pearly everlasting—and tie them together with a very narrow satin ribbon in a muted or matching color. Sage green and beige are appropriate with most combinations. Tie the ribbon in a bow and then add a loop for hanging. These can decorate a window sash on the shady side of the house or be hung from cabinet knobs.

© Derek Fell

BRAIDED GARLAND

Easier to make than a solid-rope garland of flowers, a raffia garland does not hang quite as softly, but is otherwise a good substitute. To make it hang more gracefully, simply shape it into the curve you want after it is completed. These garlands are very attractive on a harvest buffet table or placed around a door or window. To make sharp changes in direction, as for the corners of a window, make separate braids: one curved for the top and two straight ones of equal length for the sides. At the corners where they join, cover the ends with a nosegay of strawflowers.

Materials:

- Raffia in very long strands
- Dried flowers with short stems (wired into small bundles and attached to florist picks)
- Florist picks
- Florist tape in buff shade

Begin with a bundle of raffia about the diameter you wish your finished braid to be. Tie it near one end and braid loosely. When the braid begins to feel smaller, add more raffia by braiding in several strands at a time. If all the raffia is the same length, you will need to taper the bundle by cutting some of the strands to varying shorter lengths so that it does not end all at once. There should be at least 2 feet (60 cm) of difference between the lengths of the shortest and longest strands. This keeps the braid even, preventing bulges from forming when new raffia is added. Continue braiding until your garland is the length you need, then tie the final end.

Some of the bundles of dried flowers attached to picks may need to be wrapped in florist tape at the very top to cover the wire, but fuller flowers should cover it sufficiently. If strawflowers are already on wire stems, simply cut these short and tape other flowers to them for bundles. Be sure to turn the flower heads to one side, since the little bunches will lie flat with only one side showing.

Lay the garland on a flat surface, and push the bunches of flowers into the braid. Stems should go into the V of the braid and be fairly evenly spaced. The distance between them depends on how many bunches you have and the length of the garland. To hang, drive long finish nails into the top of a window or door frame where they will not show, and impale the garland on these.

To store, coil the garland in a large, flat box. If flowers become faded or damaged, they can be removed and replaced with new bundles without detracting from the braid.

A FLOWER BRAID

From the Mediterranean shores of France, Spain, and Italy comes this charming custom of decorating a kitchen with a braid of straw or raffia studded with flowers. These may have originated with the braided strings of garlic, shallots, and onions so common there.

Materials:

- Raffia bundle at least 36 inches (90 cm) long and about an inch (2.5 cm) thick
- Cinnamon stick about 6 inches (15 cm) long
- Dried flowers in bright colors, such as statice, strawflower, globe amaranth, and tansy, preferably several varieties
- White glue

Reserve two strands of raffia for later use. Fold the raffia over the cinnamon stick so that you have a fat bundle half its original length. Divide into 3 even strands and braid loosely. Be sure the braid is even so it will hang straight. Curve each loop sharply to make the braid wide and fairly flat. Leave 3 or 4 inches (about 10 cm) of tail, and tie with raffia. Trim the ends if there are any long, straggly pieces, but don't cut it straight across; you want it to look natural.

Decorate the braid with clumps of the dried flowers, grouping a large flower with several small ones or combining medium flowers. Either push their stems into the braided raffia or glue them in place. If the flowers have stems, you can gather them into little nosegays and tie them together with raffia before attaching them to the braid. Tie each end of a 12-inch (30-cm) length of raffia to an end of the cinnamon stick to form a hanging loop for the braid.

Opposite page: A small braid of raffia decorated with dried flowers adds interest to the door of a small cabinet.

Fold the raffia in half over the cinnamon stick.

Divide the raffia into thirds and begin braiding.

Opposite page: A flowered straw hat can decorate an entry hall when it is not being worn. This page: Strawflowers should be picked for drying just before they are fully open at the centers.

A FLOWERED STRAW HAT

Straw hats are the perfect base for decorating with dried flowers. When finished, a hat can be worn, or alternatively, hung on the wall or door as a bright decoration. There are hats available at florist-supply stores in small sizes, just for decorating.

Materials:

- Plain straw hat
- Ribbon—at least 1 yard (90 cm) long and 1 inch (2.5 cm) wide
- Strawflowers—about 7
- Dried flowers, leaves, or grasses
- White tacky glue

Wrap the ribbon around the crown of the hat, close to the brim. Cross it in the back, making sure that the tails are the same length. Using small dabs of glue along the bottom edge of the ribbon, glue it in place.

Working in the area where the ribbon crosses, glue the largest flowers along the ribbon, keeping the biggest one in the center and dividing the rest equally between the two sides. The design should not be exactly the same on each side, but it should be balanced. When you like your arrangement, glue the flowers in place by putting a spot of glue about the size of your thumbnail on the center of the back of each flower. Hold in place until the glue sets slightly. This will take only a few seconds.

Using smaller flowers, leaves, or grasses, fill in the spaces between the flowers and add some touches at each end to "finish off" the design. Glue these in place with tiny dots of glue on the stems.

Trim the ends of the ribbons at an angle so they won't fray. Let the hat dry overnight before wearing or hanging it.

© Robert E. Lyons

A FLOWER-TRIMMED BASKET

Nothing sets off the colors and textures of dried flowers quite like the brown and buff tones of a basket. For this project, choose a naturally colored round reed or vine basket, not one woven of wide-split ash splints. It should also have a wide, sturdy rim and handle.

Materials:

- Basket
- Assortment of everlastings, including strawflowers, statice, and grasses
- Straight pins (optional)
- Glue gun

Divide your dried material by color and size. Begin working with the larger, showier flowers, using them as focal points on the rim of the basket. Hold them in place as you experiment with arrangements, or anchor them temporarily with pins. On a small basket, you might want to have only 2 principal groupings of flowers, centered at either handle. A larger basket would look better with several groupings, giving it a less precise, more casual look.

When you have the basic design of the larger flowers established, glue them in place. Add the other flowers, filling in and letting them extend over the edge. If the basket is to be used as a gift container, keep the decorations to the outer edge. If your main flower groupings are at the base of the handle, you can extend the decorations a short way up the handles as well. Finally, add grass seed heads at the edges of the groupings to blend them together more smoothly.

A FLOWERED FAN

Graceful fan-shaped baskets can be formed from round, flat, woven palm fans. Look for these in basket shops or at florist-supply stores.

Materials:

- Palm fan
- Warm water
- Medium gauge florist wire
- Assortment of dried flowers in pink, maroon, and gray shades, such as strawflowers, statice, artemisia, celosia, marjoram, sage, and bay leaves
- Rosebuds in pink shade (wired in small bunches to florist picks)
- Florist picks
- White glue
- Ribbon in pink shade (optional)

At least a day ahead, soak the face of the fan in warm water until you are able to bend it without breaking it. Fold the bottom toward the handle to form a semicircle, but do not bend it exactly in half. There should be about an inch (2.5 cm) between the back rim and the front one, forming a pocket with a higher back. Secure the front edge to the base of the handle with a piece of wire running through both layers and twisted together in the back.

Bend the stems of the strawflowers so that the flowers face forward. Beginning with the largest flowers, arrange them in a fan shape against the back wall of the pocket. Add smaller material, working down and forward. Glue flowers in place against the back and each other if you need to. When you have a design that is balanced, add the artemisia, bay, and sage leaves as accents and to fill in bare places. Glue a single blossom at the base of the handle to cover the wire.

Opposite page: A flower-filled fan arrangement can hang on the wall or stand against a background.

Soak the center of a woven palm fan until it is soft enough to bend upward.

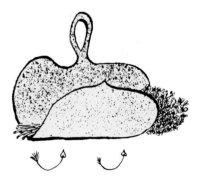

If the fan is large, you may need to begin by laying some full-shaped dried flowers in the bottom as a base for the others.

A POTPOURRI BOX

Potpourri, in order to retain its elusive scent, should be kept in a container that can be covered for at least as many hours a day as it is left open. This resting time allows a potpourri to recoup its strength, and it will last much longer that way. What better container for your own fragrant blends of potpourri than this box, which echoes its contents and is as lovely when closed as your potpourri when open.

Opposite page: Since potpourri should be kept covered half the time to recoup its scent, a covered box decorated with dried flowers makes the perfect container.

Materials:

- Round Shaker-style wooden box with lid
- Dried flowers, including 1 large, perfectly round strawflower, unstemmed
- White glue
- Small pressed leaves, such as uva ursi, bay, or dusty miller, proportionate to the size of the box and flowers used

Place the large strawflower in the exact center of the box lid, and anchor it with a drop of glue. Working outward in circles, continue to add flowers to the arrangement, keeping it balanced for color and texture. Use the very smallest flowers at the edge. When the flowers are arranged and glued in place, add accents with the leaves.

If you have dusty miller leaves, you can make a base of these radiating out from the center of the box like a lace edge and build your arrangement over them so that they show under it at the edges. If some of the flowers stand up higher than the strawflower, you can raise it slightly by putting a small support of cardboard under it.

Opposite page: Decorate a heart-shaped box as a container for Valentine potpourri, hand-dipped chocolates, or a small gift. This page: The deep red of strawflowers grows even richer as they dry.

© Rogers Associates

A VALENTINE BOX

Hearts and flowers combine on this box to hold a Valentine gift—perhaps a pink-and-red potpourri. Take the flowers to the store with you so you can match the ribbon. This type of box is available at hobby shops.

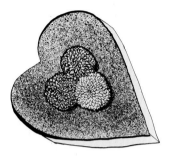

Place the three large flowers in the center to follow the contours of the heart.

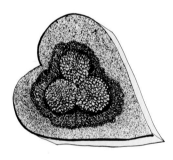

Surround the flowers with gathered lace.

Cover the edge of the box with ribbon, with the seam inside the V at the top.

Materials:

- Heart-shaped basswood box with cover
- White lace, narrow and tightly gathered
- Strawflowers—2 of matching sizes and 1 slightly smaller in deep red shade
- White glue
- Rosebuds—3 in pink shade
- Pearly everlasting, baby's breath, or white statice florets, enough to fill in the spaces between the other flowers
- Satin ribbon, in shade matching roses or strawflowers

Place the strawflowers on the box lid with the 2 larger ones toward the round sides of the heart and the smaller flower toward the point. Be sure this "heart" of strawflowers is perfectly centered and glue the flowers in place.

Surround the flowers with the lace ruffle, tucking the ends of the lace into the V at the top between the two larger flowers. The outside edge of the ruffle should follow the shape of the outer rim of the box as much as possible. Glue lace in place, taking care to keep the V pointed at the top of the heart.

Glue 3 rosebuds in the spaces between the strawflowers, making sure their stems are tucked under the strawflower petals. Fill in with white flowers to cover the inside edges of the lace and smooth up the outline of the design.

Cover the edge of the lid with the satin ribbon, clipping the ends to fit perfectly inside the V at the top and pinching a crease in the ribbon to correspond with the point at the bottom. Spread the glue very thinly, a small space at a time along the edge of the box, and press the ribbon in place carefully.

A BALL OF FLOWERS

Made of delicate flowers on a small sphere, this ball of flowers makes a lovely Christmas tree ornament. Made with bigger flowers on a larger ball, it can be a stunning centerpiece for an entire room. By varying the colors of the flowers, it can become a decoration for any season—deep reds and white for Christmas, russets and yellows for autumn, or soft pastels for spring.

Opposite page: A ball of red globe amaranth and strawflowers can be made small enough for a Christmas tree ornament or larger to highlight a window.

Materials:

- Papier mâché ball or plastic egg (see "Tools and Supplies," page 29)
- Satin ribbon—6 to 8 inches (15–20 cm) long, ¼ inch (6 mm) wide in a shade matching flowers
- Drinking glass
- Strawflowers or globe amaranth in sizes proportional to the sphere (a small ball loses its shape if covered by large flowers)
- Small flowers, such as baby's breath, pearly everlasting, or florets of statice
- Glue gun or tacky glue

In order to keep the sphere from rolling away, rest it on the mouth of the drinking glass. Make a loop of the ribbon, and glue it to the sphere to form a hanger. Cover the entire sphere with strawflowers or globe amaranth, placing them as close together as possible without crushing them. When the ball is completely covered, fill in any leftover spaces with the smaller flowers.

© Joanne Pavia

A FLOWER CROWN

This traditional May Day crown has been worn for centuries by European girls while dancing around maypoles. Crowns of flowers still add a festive note to a spring or summer party. When created with pink rosebuds and white flowers, they are perfect for a wedding.

Be very careful with the details of a flower crown, since it will be seen at close range.

Attach bundles of dried flowers so that each bunch covers the stems of the one before it.

Materials:

- Medium-weight florist wire
- Florist tape in green or white colors
- Dried flowers in sprigs at least 2 inches (5 cm) long, about 30–40
- Rosebuds (wired in small bunches to florist picks—optional)
- Ribbons—three 2-foot- (60-cm-) long pieces in shade matching flowers (optional)

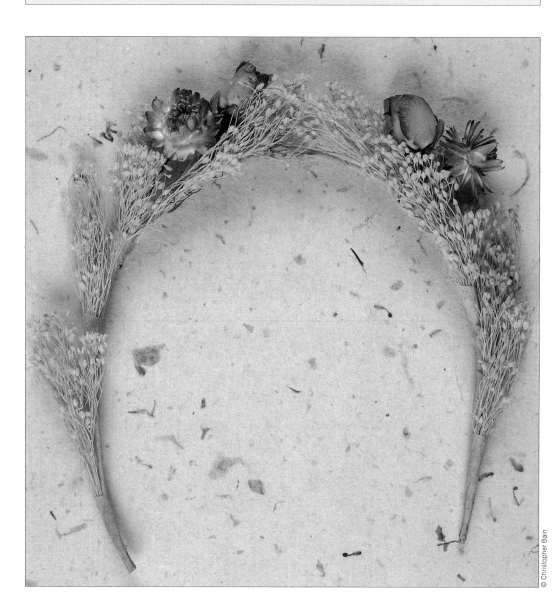

Bend the wire into a circle and try it on. Adjust it to a comfortable size and loop or twist the wire together to hold it in place. Wrap the entire ring with florist tape, stretching it as you wrap.

Gather the flowers into little bunches with tops about an inch (2.5 cm) wide, and wrap the stems together with florist tape. Be sure to make an even number of bunches of each color. If you are using rosebuds wired to florist picks, cut the picks to 2 inches (5 cm) long. You will need 12 to 16 of these little bunches of flowers, including the roses.

Begin at the center of the front of the crown (exactly opposite of the point where the wires join), and place a bundle of flowers along the frame with the flowers pointing toward the center and the stems lying directly along the wire frame. Attach it to the frame with 2 or 3 wraps of tape. When you do this, be sure to lay aside another bunch of flowers in the same colors so you can complete the other side in a matching sequence. Continue to add bundles, working back along the wire, with the bundles overlapping to form a full band of flowers along the ring. Keep the flowers to the top and outside of the ring, not the inside. This allows the taped wire to rest on the hair, which keeps the crown in place.

When the flowers cover about a quarter of the frame, end the tape and begin again at the center, working in the other direction and matching the order of the flower colors. (Crowns may be made with flowers all the way around, but they are a little harder to keep in place when worn. To make a full crown, you will need 24 to 36 bunches of flowers.)

If using ribbons, stack them with the ends even, and fold the stack in half. Place the loop made by this fold across the center of the very back of the crown and bring ribbon tails through the loop. Trim the ends evenly, cutting them at an angle to prevent fraying.

© Derek Fell

HAIR NOSEGAYS

*Miniature tussie-mussies, surrounded by a frill of lace, make a dainty
addition to the hairdo of a little girl (or a big girl). • Although we do not
encourage the use of polystyrene, if it is from recycled grocery-store meat
packaging, it can be used with a clearer conscience. Otherwise, a small disk of
heavy paper makes an acceptable substitute.*

Push wire hairpin through base.

Push stems of tiny rosebuds into base as close together as possible.

Surround the roses with narrow gathered lace to cover the edge.

Materials:

- Polystyrene sheet or heavy white paper, about 1 inch (2.5 cm) square for each nosegay
- Hairpins
- White glue
- Small rosebuds—about 6 to 8 for each nosegay
- White lace, narrow and gathered—about 4 inches (10 cm) for each
- Whole cloves
- Satin picot ribbon, ¼ inch (6 mm) wide, about 10 inches (25 cm) for each
- Typing paper

Cut the polystyrene sheet or paper into circles each about the size of a nickel. Push the end of the hairpin through the center of the circle, and secure it from the top with a drop of glue.

From the other side, push the stems of several small rosebuds through the disk, as close together as possible. They should almost fill the disk, but not be close enough to the edge to rip it. Touch a drop of glue to the backs of the buds and let it dry slightly.

Glue a ruffle of white lace around the outer edge, and when the glue has dried, cover any visible edges, and fill in bare spaces with whole cloves.

Snip off any stems that have pushed too far through the back, and cover the back with a disk of polystyrene or white typing paper. Make a bow with long streamers, and glue it to 1 edge of the top of the nosegay.

In fine or straight hair, it may be helpful to secure the wires of the hairpin underneath a small, plain barrette to hold the nosegay in place.

© Derek Fell

AN ARTEMISIA TREE

*Tabletop trees are made from sprigs of artemisia or other foliage pushed into a
cone made of fine chicken wire. Once the basic tree form is made, it can be
decorated with any dried flowers you like, simply by pushing their stems into
the foliage or into the cone itself.   •   If you live in a climate where there
are large quantities of rosemary available, you can use that herb in place
of the artemisia. The finished tree will look even more like a fir tree and
will remain fragrant for months.*

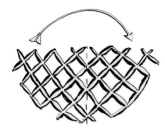

Fold chicken wire into a cone shape.

Begin the tree at the bottom, pushing stems upward into the wire mesh.

Use shorter sprigs at the top to simulate the pointed tip of a fir tree.

Materials:

- Small-gauge chicken wire screen, 18 × 36 inches (45 × 90 cm)
- Wire cutters
- Florist tape
- Artemisia tips, fresh or dried—about 50 if full, more if sparse
- Assortment of dried flowers for decorating, such as strawflowers, statice, globe amaranth, and lavender—in single or mixed color scheme
- White glue or glue gun

Cut the chicken wire into a semicircle with the wire cutters. Fold the straight side in half to form a cone, overlapping more for a narrow tree and less for a wider one. Twist the wire ends into the mesh to hold the cone in shape.

Wrap the bottom edges with florist tape, stretching it as you work. Check the tree to be sure it stands straight.

Beginning at the bottom, push short lengths of artemisia into the cone, with the stems pointing upward inside the cone and the tips curving downward like the branches of a fir tree. Continue working up the sides of the cone, using slightly shorter stems as you work. At the top of the cone, you will run out of space inside. Using a very short tip, form a tree top by pushing it straight down into the point. Fill in with short pieces of artemisia pointed up and outward. You can fill in any rough places with "ornaments" later.

Decorate the tree with an assortment of dried flowers as you would a Christmas tree, balancing their sizes, shapes, and colors for a harmonious blend.

At the very top, you might place 2 bright yellow strawflowers of the same size back to back and glue in place.

Opposite page: Small nosegays in Christmas colors add life to
decorative greens. This page: Globe
amaranth.

© Derek Fell

CHRISTMAS NOSEGAYS

These are so simple and so versatile that you will want to make them not only as tree ornaments, but to decorate packages, tuck into gift baskets, or use as table decorations and favors. A shallow basket filled with nosegays on the hall table not only decorates, but provides lovely little gifts for your guests as they leave. Plant material amounts given are for a single nosegay, so increase volume accordingly for several nosegays.

Small nosegays in shades of pink are appropriate for springtime decorations.

Lay the bundle of flowers on a square of tissue paper.

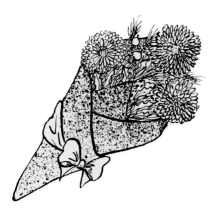

Bring the corners up to surround the flowers and cover the stems.

Materials:

- Strawflower—1 small red blossom on a 4-to 6-inch (10- to 15 cm-) wire stem

- Baby's breath—one 6-inch (15-cm) sprig

- White annual statice—one 6-inch (15-cm) stem

- Assortment of dried flowers—2 or 3 small varieties on 6-inch (15-cm) stems in red, green, white, or gold shades

- Tissue paper—6 inches (15 cm) square in green, red, or white shades

- Picot ribbon—12 inches (30 cm) long and ¼ inch (6 mm) wide in red, green, or white shades (to contrast with or match paper)

- Fine-gauge florist wire

- Heavy scissors

Begin with the strawflower, baby's breath, and statice, holding them together in a bundle. Select 2 or 3 other flowers with colors and shapes that complement those of the first flowers. Add these, arranging them in the bundle so they don't crowd it. Tie the stems together, about halfway down, with a short piece of florist wire.

Clip all the stems except the wire, so that the bundle is about 4 to 5 inches (10 to 12.5 cm) long. Bend the wire upward to make it the same length and to prevent it from piercing the tissue.

Wrap the nosegay in the tissue so that 3 of the corners frame the flowers, pinching the tissue close to the stems about halfway up. Tie the ribbon around the stems and tissue at this point, making a neat bow.

If you are making a number of these at one time, it is easier to spread all the flowers out in front of you and make all the bundles at once. Then spread out the tissue and ribbons and finish them all.

To make these bouquets for Easter, May Day, or a shower or other party, use pastel or other appropriately colored flowers in any combination. Choose complementary ribbon and tissue.

Dried Flower Projects • **107**

TINY TUSSIE-MUSSIES

Miniature tussie-mussies, tiny nosegays of dried flowers surrounded by lace ruffles, are a legacy of Victorian Christmas trees. These can be used with cornucopiae and tiny fans as well as other elegant decorations of the period for a parlor tree. See note on page 32 regarding the use of polystyrene.

Opposite page: Rosebuds are excellent flowers to use in projects as they retain both color and scent.

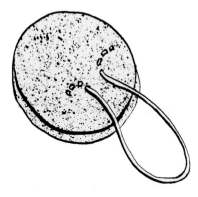

Push the bent wire through the base to make a handle.

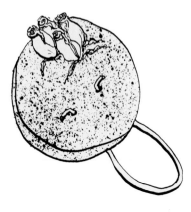

Push rose stems into the base as close together as possible.

Materials:

- Polystyrene sheet or heavy white paper, about 8 inches (20 cm) square
- Florist wire
- Rosebuds—6 to 8 for each
- White glue
- White lace, narrow and gathered
- Baby's breath, statice florets, whole cloves and uva ursi leaves
- Florist tape
- Satin picot ribbon, ¼ inch (6 mm) wide, 10 inches (25 cm) for each nosegay
- Nylon thread
- Typing paper

Cut the polystyrene or paper sheet into circles each about the size of a nickel coin. Cut a 4-inch (10-cm) length of florist wire and bend it in half. Push the ends through the center of the circle, and bend the ends over like a staple to hold it in place to form a handle.

From the other side, push the stems of several small rosebuds through the disk, as close together as possible. They should almost fill the disk, but not be close enough to the edge to rip it. Touch glue to the back (the handle side), and let it dry slightly.

Glue a ruffle of white lace around the outer edge. When the glue has dried, cover any visible edges, and fill in bare spaces with statice florets, whole cloves, or tiny leaves of ursa uvi.

Snip off any stems that have pushed too far through the back, and cover the back with a disk of typing paper. Wrap the stem with florist tape, and tie a length of ribbon around it, making a bow with long streamers. Add a loop of nylon thread glued in place for a hanger.

These tussie-mussies also make good boutonnieres and can be worn as a tiny corsage held in place by a map pin or common pin.

© Charles Mann

STRAWFLOWER TUSSIE FOR THE TREE

This miniature tussie for the Christmas tree uses scraps of lace and ribbon and could not be simpler to make. A number of them can be used to decorate a Victorian tabletop tree.

Materials:

- Fine lace—8 inches (20 cm) long and ³/₄ inch (2 cm) wide in white or off-white shade

- Ribbon—8 inches (20 cm) long and very narrow in white or off-white shade

- Heavy paper—cut in 1¹/₂-inch (3.2-cm) circles, in white or off-white shade

- White glue

- Strawflower—1 perfectly round piece in red, magenta, or pink shade

Opposite page: A single red strawflower is just the right size to be used alone in a miniature tussie.

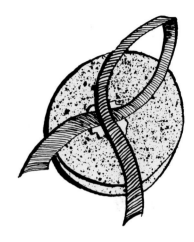

Glue a loop of ribbon to the base as a hanger.

Make a loop from the ribbon, with its ends crossed in the center (see diagram), and glue it to the center of one of the circles of paper. Gather the lace so it forms a circle with a center that is smaller than the strawflower. Carefully glue the lace over the ribbon, and then glue the strawflower in place on top of that, centering both. Hold arrangement in place until glue sets.

TINY TREE BOUQUETS

So light and airy that they seem to float on the tree, these bouquets are set on top of the branches instead of suspended from them. Short stems of very small flowers work best for these.

Materials:

- Dried flowers with stems—3 to 4 small sprigs no longer than 2.5 inches (7 cm), including stems
- Nylon net, 4 inches (10 cm) square in white
- Satin ribbon—8 inches (20 cm) long and very narrow in white or off-white shade

Gather 3 or 4 stems of the tiny flowers into a bundle. Lay the flowers on the net, with the ends of the stems in the exact center and bring the net edges up around the bouquet. Tie it 1 inch (2.5 cm) from the bottom of the bouquet with the ribbon, making a neat bow. Trim ribbon ends evenly.

WALNUT SHELL ORNAMENTS

Walnut shells make the perfect basket for an arrangement of miniature dried flowers. Save the very smallest strawflowers and the single florets that break off the statice you used for other projects. A single wisp of plume celosia, a tansy button, or a floret of yarrow is large enough for filler in these.

Opposite page: Walnut shells hold arrangements made of the tiniest flowers, often a single floret out of a larger blossom.

Fill the cavity of the walnut shell with a cotton ball.

Materials:

- Satin ribbon—2 inches (5 cm) long and very narrow
- Walnut shells in perfect halves
- Cotton balls
- White glue
- Tiny strawflowers, globe amaranth, and other flowers and florets in limited color range (5 or 6 for each walnut)

Make a loop of ribbon and glue it into the rounded end of the walnut shell so it extends over the top. Cut a cotton ball in half, and push it into the cavity of the walnut shell. It should not quite fill the shell. If it fills it to the rim, remove the cotton and cut it down more. Spread the top of the cotton very thinly with glue, press down to smooth it, and allow to dry slightly.

On this base, arrange the flowers, using 1 strawflower near the top and filling in with the others. Since these flowers are so small, it is best to stick to a small range of colors, such as yellows and oranges, pinks and whites. Although these decorations are small, they are surprisingly sturdy and will last for many years if they are handled gently and stored in egg cartons.

© Rogers Associates

DRIED FLOWER POTPOURRI

*Along with their beautiful colors and shapes, you can preserve the fresh,
heady scents of flowers by drying them. For example, when dried old rose
varieties emit their fragrance almost as sweetly as when they were fresh.
Lavender flowers also retain their crisp, clean scent when dried. While not all
flowers dry as well as these examples, the flower garden will yield enough
fragrant plants to produce a good blend for a potpourri.*

Place larger, showy flowers around the edge, facing out, and fill behind them with potpourri.

Rose, lavender, chamomile, orange blossom, lemon marigold, jasmine, lime flower, heather, and carnation all have good fragrance when dried. Some herbs, such as mint, lemon balm, lemon verbena, tansy, bergamot, sweet fern, and the scented geranium, are also highly fragrant.

Ingredients from the kitchen shelf can be added for spicy overtones and a delicate herbal touch. Cinnamon sticks, whole cloves and allspice, thyme, rosemary, mint, marjoram, and bay leaves can be used alone or blended with flowers. Be sure to save all your orange and lemon peels, which can be cut into strips and dried to add a piquant touch to spicy or floral potpourris.

While scent is the most important consideration in potpourri, it is not the only one. Color is important if the blend is to be displayed in a glass jar or open container, so bright blossoms should be included. Bulk is provided by larger whole flowers, which also create air spaces so the fragrances can move about and blend. Some flowers, such as whole pink roses, suit all these needs.

Potpourri is the project that will use all those bits and pieces—broken tips, shattered flowers, and lost petals—that you've been collecting as you work with

dried flowers. Even overbloomed strawflowers and slightly faded blossoms blend easily into a potpourri, where the effect is created by the combination, not by a single flower. Strawflowers and globe amaranth add bulk and color, as do the tips of statice, plume celosia, yarrow, tansy, artemisia, and baby's breath. Whole flowers can be added at the top.

When the potpourri smells and looks good, it is time to consider preserving and strengthening its scent. Orris, the dried root of the Florentine iris, is the best fixative, and should be used chipped, not powdered. It has no scent of its own, but helps others to last.

Since drying has evaporated some of the fragrant oils in the flowers, it is best to replace these with essential oils. Rose is the most versatile of these, blending well with nearly any other fragrance. Lavender is the strongest and tends to dominate others. Bay, balsam, cedar, orange, lemon, gardenia, and carnation are also favorites, but since good oils are quite expensive, it is best to begin with just a few and add more if you find you enjoy creating potpourri.

Much of the fun of making potpourri lies in experimenting with your own original blends of colors and fragrances. There are no firm rules; there are no

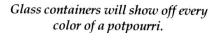

Glass containers will show off every color of a potpourri.

flowers that you cannot mix, so no matter how wildly you experiment, you won't get a bad blend.

There is also no magic about the quantities. Mix your ingredients in whatever amount you have or like, and add 1 or 2 tablespoons (15 or 30 ml) of orris root per pint (.5 l) of flowers. Depending on the intended use for the potpourri, use 4 to 8 drops of oil to a pint. Mix well and seal in a jar with plenty of air space. Shake or stir it daily for 2 weeks to allow it to blend and ripen. After that, your potpourri is ready.

To make potpourri last longer, keep it covered for as many hours a day as it is left open. Many people close the jar or cover the dish at night, opening it each morning. Like anything else made of dried flowers, potpourri will lose both color and scent if left in the sun. If the fragrance fades, simply treat it as you would a brand new mix—add orris root and oil and let it blend in a large jar for 2 weeks.

Although you will soon be creating your own blends of potpourri from whatever materials you have on hand, the following "recipes" will get you started. Add whatever else you might have, leave out what you don't have, and keep experimenting to come up with unique blends that are entirely yours.

Rose Potpourri

- 1 cup (.25 l) dried rose buds and petals
- 1 cup (.25 l) mixed pink and white dried flowers
- ¼ cup (60 ml) rosemary leaves
- ¼ cup (60 ml) broken stick cinnamon
- ¼ cup (60 ml) bay leaves
- 1 tbsp. (15 ml) whole cloves
- 3 tbsp. (45 ml) orris root chips
- 6 to 8 drops rose oil

Lavender Potpourri

- 1 cup (.25 l) lavender flowers
- ½ cup (.12 l) roses
- ½ cup (.12 l) blue and white flowers
- 1 tbsp. (15 ml) lemon peel
- 2 tbsp. (30 ml) orris root chips
- 4 to 6 drops lavender oil

Scotch Heather

- ½ cup (.12 l) heather flowers
- ½ cup (.12 l) pink roses
- 1 cup (.25 l) artemisia leaves and tips
- 1 cup (.25 l) pink and light rose dried flowers
- ½ cup bay leaves
- 3 tbsp. (45 ml) orris root chips
- 6 to 8 drops of rose oil

Displaying your blends of dried flowers is as much fun as making the potpourri. Containers with covers that can be removed during the day are the best, and since your blends are as beautiful as they are fragrant, it's nice to have a container that shows them off.

Glass rose bowls, the clear glass vases shaped like crystal balls, make good containers because they have so much surface.

Pour a little potpourri into the rose bowl—no more than 2 inches (5 cm) deep—and carefully arrange flat, well-opened strawflowers around the sides, facing the glass. Leave enough space between them to allow the potpourri to show through. Pour more potpourri into the center to hold them in place, and repeat with more layers until the bowl is full. Top with one perfect strawflower. Set the rose bowl on a flat clear glass plate for display, and use the plate as a cover at night.

Transparent Lucite boxes are good potpourri containers, especially for gifts. They can even be wrapped and mailed without damage. If the potpourri is packed more firmly than usual, an arrangement of perfect flowers on top will stay in place.

Fill the box almost full and press perfect strawflowers, rosebuds, bay leaves, or globe amaranth blossoms into an arrangement on the top. When the lid is down, it should hold the flowers in place. Tie a matching ribbon around the box to hold the lid in place for gift giving.

SOURCES

Plants and seeds for drying flowers:

Alberta Nurseries and Seed, Ltd.
P.O. Box 20
Bowden, Alberta T0M 0K0 Canada

Goodwin Creek Gardens
P.O. Box 83
Williams, Oregon 97544
(Catalog 50¢, specializing in everlastings)

Jackson and Perkins Co.
P.O. Box 1028
Medford, Oregon 97501
(Roses)

Richters
P.O. Box 26C Goodwood
Ontario L0C 1A0 Canada
(Catalog $2.50, large selection)

Shepherd's Garden Seeds
6116 Highway 9
Felton, California 95018

Andre Viette Farm and Nursery
Route 1, Box 16
Fishersville, Virginia 22939
(Catalog $2.00, wide selection of unusual
    everlastings)

Supplies and dried flowers:

Cramer's Posy Patch
Box 429A, RD 2
Columbia, Pennsylvania 17512
(Wide variety of flowers; wholesale, but
    with low enough minimum order for
    individuals to meet)

Flag Fork Herb Farm
260 Flag Fork Road
Frankfort, Kentucky 40601
(Dried flowers, retail)

Herbitage Farm
686 Old Homestead Highway
Richmond, New Hampshire 03470
(Catalog $1.00, short-stemmed flower assort-
    ments for wreaths and glued crafts;
    books on dried flowers)

Homestead Gardens
Pumpkin Hill Road
Warner, New Hampshire 03278
(Dried flowers and grasses)

Natural Gardens
8500 Nature Lane
Columbia, Missouri 65202
(Dried flowers)

For further information and ideas:

POTPOURRI FROM HERBAL ACRES
Pine Row Publications
Box 428
Washington Crossing, Pennsylvania
    18977
(Newsletter with craft instructions and
    sources of supplies)

A

Achillea 14

Adhesives 32

African daisy 19

Agrostis 17

Air drying 23

Allspice 120

Anaphalis 17

Artemisia 14, 101, 120

B

Baby's Breath 15, 26, 120

Balsam 120

Bases 31

Basket 37, 79

Bay leaves 26, 120, 123

Bouquet 59, 63, 115

Braided garland 69

C

Calluna vulgaris 17

Carnation 120

Cedar 120

Celosia 15

Centaurea rutifolia 18

Chamomile 120

Chinese lantern 16

Christmas nosegay 105

Cinnamon 120

Cone-shaped base 31

Cortaderia 18

Crown 93

D

Displaying potpourri 123

Drying flowers 23, 24

Dusty miller 18

F

Fan, flowered 83

Filipendula Hexapetala 19

Florentine iris 120

Florist tape 33

Flowers for wreaths 50

Fragrant oils 120

Frames 32

G

Globe amaranth 120, 123

Glue 32, 33

Glycerine preserving 25

Gnaphalium 19

Goldenrod 21

Gomphrena 15

Grasses 17

Gypsophila 15

H

Hair nosegay 97

Hanging flowers 66

Harvesting 13

Hat decorated with flowers 75

Heart-shaped box 88

Heather 16, 17, 120

Helichrysum 16

Helipterum 19

J

Jasmine 120

L

Lamb's ears 21

Lavandula officinalis 20

Lavender 20, 120

    Oil 120

    Potpourri 122

Lemon balm 120

    peel 120

    verbena 120

Lime flowers 120

Limonium 16

M

Marjoram 20, 120

May Day crown 93

Meadowsweet 19

Mint 120

N

Nosegays 97, 105

O

Oasis 30, 31

Oats 17

Oils 120

Orange 120

Origanum vulgare 20

P

Palm fan 83

Pampas grass 18

Panicum 17

Papier mâché bases 31, 91

Pearly everlasting 17

Physalis 16

Planting 12

Plastic eggs 31

Plume celosia 12, 15, 120

Polystyrene 31

Potpourri 119

    box 85

Pressing flowers 24

Q

Queen Anne's Lace 18

R

Raffia 33, 73
Rosa rugosa 20
Rose 20, 26, 120, 122, 123
 Oil 120
 potpourri 122
Rosemary 120
Rye 17

S

Sand drying 25
Scented geranium 120
Scotch heather potpourri 123
Seeds 12, 25
 starting 12
Senicio cineraria 18
Shaker box 85

Silica gel 25
Solidago sempervirens 21
Stachys olimpica 21
Statice 13, 16, 26, 120
Strawflowers 13, 16, 26, 120
Supplies 29, 125
Swag 57
Sweet fern 120

T

Tanacetum vulgare 21
Tansy 13, 21, 120
Thyme 120
Tools 29
Transplanting 12

U

Ursa Uvi 26

V

Valentine box 87
Victorian ornaments 109

W

Walnut shell ornament 117
Wheat 17
Williamsburg fan 41
Windowsill basket 45
Wire 29
Wreath, artemisia 117
 bases 32
 frames 32

Y

Yarrow 13, 14, 120